HOW TO MEASURE

Weight

Beth Bence Reinke

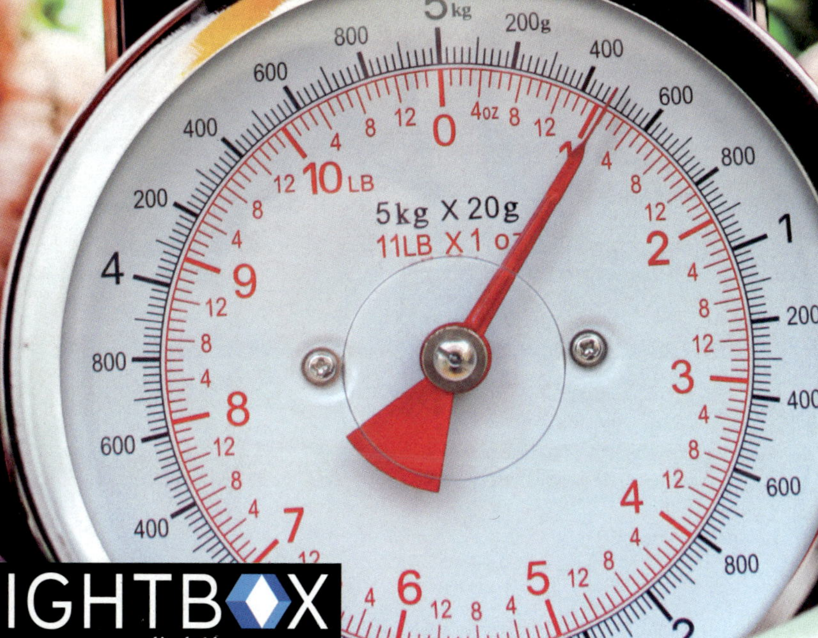

LIGHTBOX
openlightbox.com

Go to
www.openlightbox.com
and enter this book's
unique code.

ACCESS CODE

LBN24278

Lightbox is an all-inclusive digital solution for the teaching and learning of curriculum topics in an original, groundbreaking way. Lightbox is based on National Curriculum Standards.

STANDARD FEATURES OF LIGHTBOX

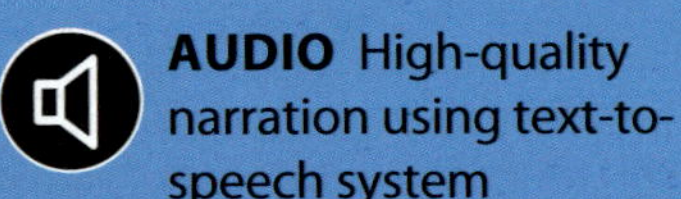

AUDIO High-quality narration using text-to-speech system

ACTIVITIES Printable PDFs that can be emailed and graded

SLIDESHOWS Pictorial overviews of key concepts

VIDEOS Embedded high-definition video clips

WEBLINKS Curated links to external, child-safe resources

TRANSPARENCIES Step-by-step layering of maps, diagrams, charts, and timelines

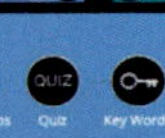

INTERACTIVE MAPS Interactive maps and aerial satellite imagery

QUIZZES Ten multiple choice questions that are automatically graded and emailed for teacher assessment

KEY WORDS Matching key concepts to their definitions

Contents

What Is Weight?

How much does Mia's kitten weigh? It's hard to tell by holding it. The vet uses a **scale** to measure the kitten's weight. Weight is how heavy something is.

Healthy kittens will double their weight between 6 and 12 months of age.

The kitten's weight goes up as it grows. Mia gains weight as she grows, too. So do you!

It's fun to measure weight. We can weigh tiny things like paper clips. We can weigh big things like desks. You can even weigh your favorite grown-up.

Keeping track of weight is important for staying healthy.

The world's **smallest** bat weighs the same as **two paper clips**.

A person would **weigh** about **twice** as much on **Jupiter** and half as much on **Mars**.

A **baby blue whale** is **20** times **heavier** than an adult **human**.

Which weighs more, a banana or an apple? How heavy is a puppy? How much does a letter weigh? You can find out. Let's measure weight!

To do the activities in this book, you will need:

- bathroom scale
- kitchen scale
- objects from around the house
- a pet, or an object from your home
- paper and pencil

Weight Timeline

3000 BC To measure weight, Egyptians and Mesopotamians see how many grains of barley it takes to weigh about the same as the object being measured.

400–1400 AD During the Middle Ages, grains of barley are still used around the world to find weight. Even money, in coins, is measured by weighing.

1770 Richard Salter of Great Britain makes the first **spring scale**. The scales used in homes today are still modeled after it.

1790 French scientists work on a more **uniform** way of measuring weight. They decide weight should be compared to a specific amount of water at a certain temperature.

1850 During the Gold Rush, California passes a law to make a uniform system for weight. This helps the buying and selling of gold stay fair.

1980s Digital scales, which work like a small computer and use batteries, are invented. Most homes now have bathroom scales for tracking body weight.

2017 The National Aeronautics and Space Administration (NASA) announces a detailed plan for sending people to Mars. Scientists are studying how weight works in outer space and on other planets. Spaceships have to weigh as little as possible to save fuel.

Which Is Heavier?

Kids should eat two servings of fruit per day. One serving weighs as much as a baseball.

Mia and Lee are playing at the park. They packed fruit for a snack. Which weighs more, the apple or the banana?

It's hard to guess by looking at them. Mia holds one fruit in each hand. It's still hard to tell which is heavier.

A **balance** compares weights of things. The heavier object goes down. The lighter object goes up. It balances if the two objects are equal. Now can you tell which fruit is heavier?

People often think that a larger object will weigh more than a smaller object.

A seesaw works like a balance. Lee's end goes down. That is because he is heavier than Mia.

Mia goes up. She is lighter than Lee. But we still do not know how much they weigh. We need a scale to measure weight.

To play on a seesaw, kids have to work together. They have to work harder if there is a big difference in their weight.

Activity

Pretend You Are a Balance

Which things are heavier or lighter than a can of soup?

1. Gather items from your house. Some ideas are: banana, pen, book, flashlight, quarter, pair of jeans, hammer, and toothbrush.
2. Draw a line down the middle of a piece of paper. At the top, write "lighter" and "heavier."
3. Pick up each object. Guess whether it is lighter or heavier than the can of soup.
4. Now hold a small can of soup in one hand. Hold another object in the other hand. Is it lighter or heavier?
5. Write the object in the correct column.

Using Units

The price of mailing a package depends on its weight, size, and how far it is going.

We use pounds or kilograms to measure heavy things. Pounds and kilograms are **units** of measure for weight. We measure people in pounds or kilograms.

Many fruits and vegetables are priced by how much they weigh.

Mia stops at the post office. She has a package for her grandmother and a letter to mail. The clerk weighs the package first. She puts it on a scale. The package weighs three pounds (1.4 kilograms).

We can write pounds in a shorter way. The **abbreviation** for pounds is lb.

Heavier things, such as packages, are measured in pounds or kilograms.

Other units of weight are ounces and grams. Lighter things are measured in ounces or grams. There are 16 ounces in a pound (0.5 kg).

The clerk weighs Mia's letter. It weighs one ounce. The short way to write ounces is oz. Sixteen letters would add up to one pound.

Mia's letter is light. Can you think of other light objects?

Dear
Aunt Samantha

I had a great time at the Zoo,
my favorite animal was the Toucan
some day I would like to go again

from James

In the United States, one first-class letter can weigh as much as a deck of cards.

Activity

How Many Pounds Is the Puppy?

Lee's puppy will not sit still on a scale. But Lee found a way to measure him. You can try it, too.

1. Lee steps on a bathroom scale. He writes his weight on a piece of paper.
2. Then he weighs himself holding the puppy. He writes down that number.
3. Lee subtracts to find out how much his puppy weighs.
4. Do you have a pet to weigh? If not, find something else from around your house. Maybe a basket of clothes or a pair of boots? What else can you weigh?

A large breed puppy can gain about 2.5 pounds (1.1 kg) in one week.

Two Measuring Systems

Lee and Mia shop at the market. Lee orders eight ounces (230 g) of yellow cheese. Mia asks for eight ounces (230 g) of white cheese. That makes 16 ounces of cheese. That is the same as one pound (0.5 kg).

The average American eats 30 pounds (14 kg) of cheese every year.

A worker slices the cheese. She weighs it on a scale. Lee counts 16 slices in one pound of cheese. Each slice weighs one ounce (28 g).

Ounces and pounds are units in the **U.S. customary system**. This system is one way we measure.

Foods served in delis, such as meats and cheeses, are usually sold by weight.

The world's most expensive **cheese** comes from Serbia. **One pound** (0.5 kg) costs almost **$600**.

The **heaviest chocolate bar** was made in 2011 in Great Britain. It weighed **12,770 pounds** (579 kg).

A soda can filled with the world's heaviest metal, **osmium**, would weigh almost **18 pounds** (8 kg).

SODA

Food packages sold in stores are required to list weight. The weight does not include the packaging.

We also measure with a second set of units. These units are the **metric system**. It uses grams and kilograms to measure weight. The short way to write grams is g. A paper clip weighs one gram. A kilogram is 1,000 grams. You can write kilograms as kg.

Most food packages show both ounces and grams. A gram is much smaller than an ounce. There are 28 grams in every ounce.

Activity

How Many Ounces? How Many Grams?

You can weigh things in both grams and ounces. Let's try it!

1. Gather some light objects. Some ideas are: apple, spoon, phone, tissue box, car keys, salt shaker, hairbrush. You can find other objects, too.
2. Ask a grown-up how to use the kitchen scale. Where does it show weight in ounces? Where does it show weight in grams?
3. Put each object on a kitchen scale. Write down the weight in ounces.
4. Write down the weight in grams.
5. Arrange the items from heaviest to lightest.

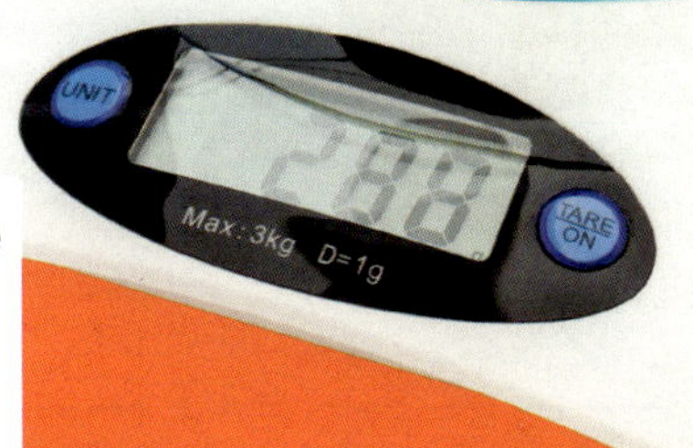

When cooking, the most accurate way to measure ingredients is to use a kitchen scale.

Record-Setting Weights

There are many record-setting weights in the United States. Some of these are the heaviest or lightest in the nation, or even in the world.

"Levitated Mass"

Los Angeles County Museum of Art, California

One of the largest boulders ever moved is part of a work of art in Los Angeles. The 340-**ton** (308-**metric ton**) boulder was moved 105 miles (170 kilometers) on a 176-wheel truck.

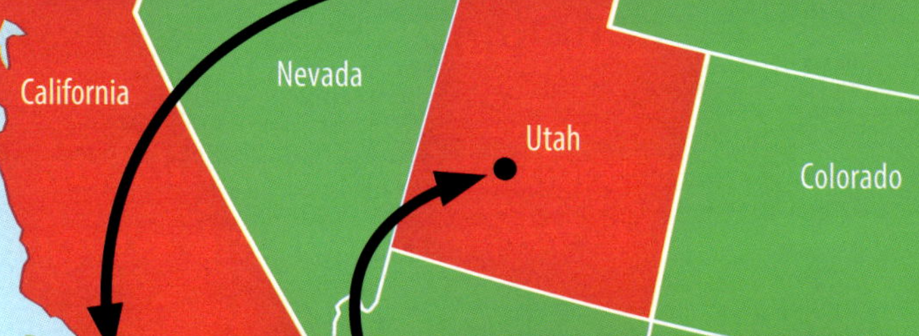

Pando Forest

Richfield, Utah

The heaviest living thing is a tree. The Pando Forest of Utah is a colony of aspen trees that weighs almost 13 million pounds (6 million kg). The trees grew from a single seed and are connected underground.

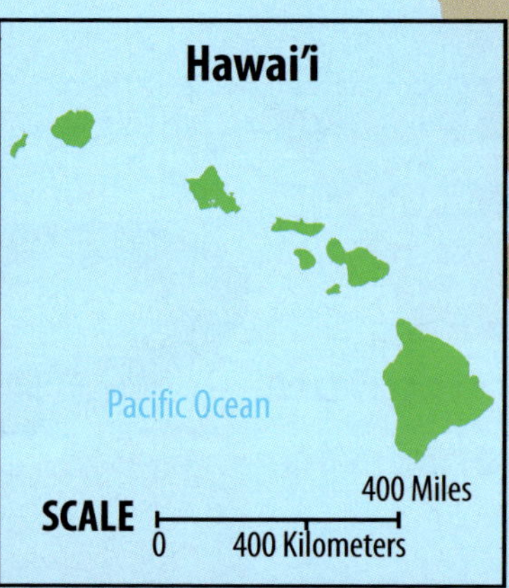

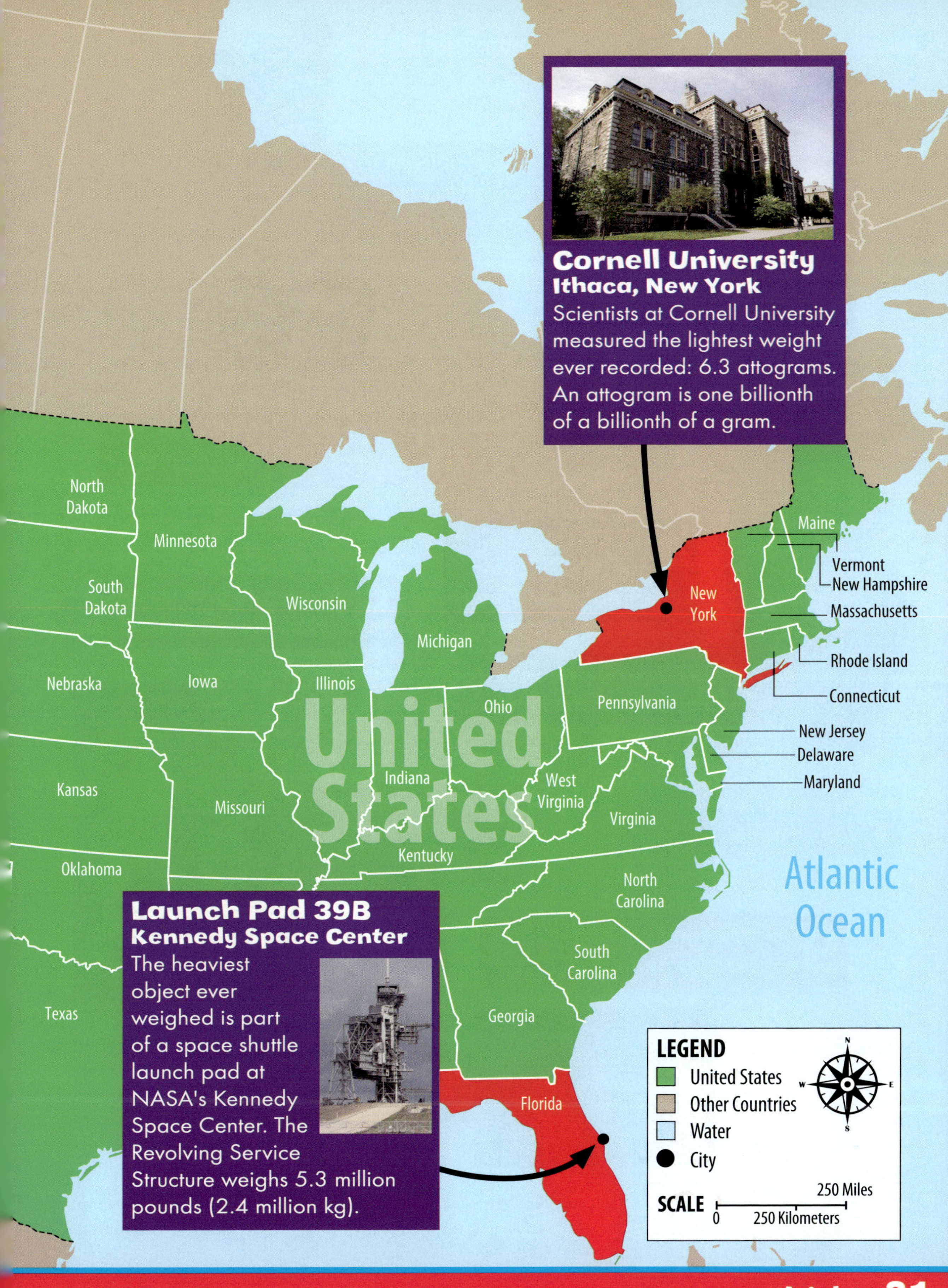

Cornell University
Ithaca, New York

Scientists at Cornell University measured the lightest weight ever recorded: 6.3 attograms. An attogram is one billionth of a billionth of a gram.

Launch Pad 39B
Kennedy Space Center

The heaviest object ever weighed is part of a space shuttle launch pad at NASA's Kennedy Space Center. The Revolving Service Structure weighs 5.3 million pounds (2.4 million kg).

Quiz

1 What tool would a vet use to measure a kitten's weight?

2 When were digital scales invented?

3 How many servings of fruit weigh as much as a baseball?

4 On a balance, does the heavier object go up or down?

5 Which playground toy works like a balance?

6 What units are used to measure heavy things?

7 What is the abbreviation for pound?

8 What units are used to measure light things?

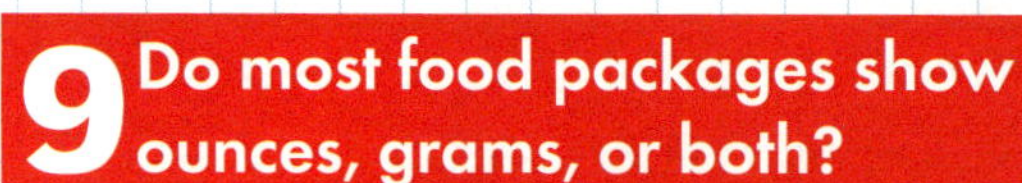

9 Do most food packages show ounces, grams, or both?

10 What is the heaviest living thing?

Answers: 1. A scale **2.** The 1980s **3.** One **4.** Down **5.** A seesaw
6. Pounds or kilograms **7.** lb **8.** Ounces or grams **9.** Both **10.** The Pando Forest

Key Words

abbreviation: a shorter form of a word

balance: a tool used to compare weights

metric system: a way to measure things based on the number ten; the gram is used to measure weight

metric ton: a unit of weight used in the metric system and equal to 2,205 pounds (1,000 kg)

scale: a device used for weighing

spring scale: a type of scale that measures weight by seeing how far down an object pulls a spring

ton: a unit of weight used in the U.S. customary system and equal to 2,000 pounds (907 kg)

uniform: when something stays the same at all times and never changes

units: standard amounts used to measure things

U.S. customary system: units of measurement typically used in the United States such as pounds, ounces, cups, quarts, miles, feet, and inches

Index

LIGHTBOX

SUPPLEMENTARY RESOURCES

Click on the plus icon found in the bottom left corner of each spread to open additional teacher resources.

- Download and print the book's quizzes and activities
- Access curriculum correlations
- Explore additional web applications that enhance the Lightbox experience

LIGHTBOX DIGITAL TITLES
Packed full of integrated media

VIDEOS

INTERACTIVE MAPS

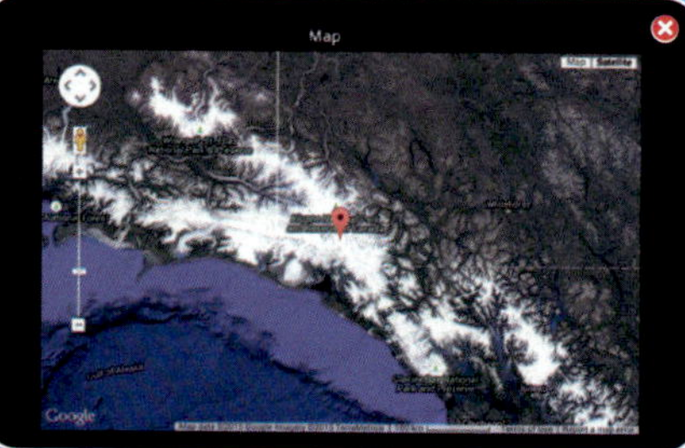

WEBLINKS

SLIDESHOWS

QUIZZES

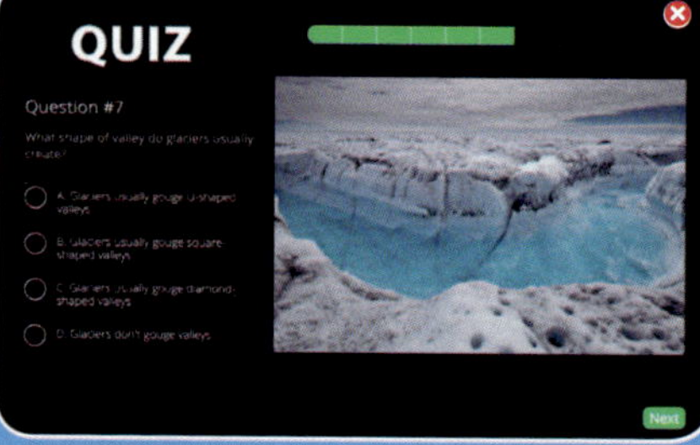

OPTIMIZED FOR

- ✓ TABLETS
- ✓ WHITEBOARDS
- ✓ COMPUTERS
- ✓ AND MUCH MORE!

Published by Smartbook Media Inc. 350 5th Avenue, 59th Floor New York, NY 10118
Website: www.openlightbox.com

012018
120517

Library of Congress Control Number: 2017960147

ISBN 978-1-5105-3628-9 (hardcover)
ISBN 978-1-5105-3629-6 (multi-user eBook)

Printed in the Brainerd, Minnesota, United States
1 2 3 4 5 6 7 8 9 0 22 21 20 19 18

First published by Cherry Lake in 2014.

Project Coordinator: John Willis
Designer: Ana María Vidal

The publisher acknowledges Alamy and Getty Images as the primary image suppliers for this title.